Finding My Way Through The Darkness

NATASHA WHITE

authorHOUSE®

AuthorHouse™ UK
1663 Liberty Drive
Bloomington, IN 47403 USA
www.authorhouse.co.uk
Phone: UK TFN: 0800 0148641 (Toll Free inside the UK)
*   UK Local: 02036 956322 (+44 20 3695 6322 from outside the UK)*

Published by AuthorHouse 01/25/2021

ISBN: 978-1-7283-5270-1 (sc)
ISBN: 978-1-7283-5269-5 (e)

Chapter 1

My earliest memory is from when I was a child of about five or six. I was ill with a sore throat, and my mother had stayed up with me all night. She sat staring out the window waiting for my father to come back with some medicine she had asked him to get for me.

He eventually returned. Getting me to take the medicine was hard, but he was very patient and concerned until I finally took it. I had the worst sickness ever. I can't express or explain how horrible it made me feel, but I was trying to make myself sick; it was so unbearable. My mother was with me the whole time, up all night with me. She was good like that—if we were ill.

That night, it was as though I was having a bad dream and was being suffocated with a pillow. I was seeing things in my head, like someone was trying to kill me. I tried to make myself sick to get rid of it.

I remember my relationship with my mother very well. Sometimes I would ask myself if she really loved me. One time I remember my brother and I were being a bit noisy in the bath. My mum came in and held my head underneath the water for what seemed like forever. I thought she did that because I was misbehaving. But she was also depressed because my dad had left and didn't come back for a long time. She did this several times. I think she was under a lot of stress. I don't believe she meant to do that.

I also remember a time when I was playing hide-and-seek with my brother. I climbed up the window, and he saw me. I fell, something smashed a glass, and I cut my wrist. My mum grabbed me and took me to my nan next door. My father came home and took me to the hospital. I just missed my artery. I could've died if it wasn't for my mother's quick thinking.

Sometimes, when it was just me and my mum, she would take me to the doctor. We would talk. It was nice to spend some time with her, and she would take me to the shops and buy me sweets. She would then make out to the doctor that there was something wrong with me. She would tell me to lie to the doctor about being ill. It was an excuse for her to ask for her slimming tablets. At times, she would sell them to get some money.

Even when my mum and dad separated, he tried his hardest to take care of us. Staying with my dad wasn't the same as staying with my mum. I know he tried his best, and I felt he loved us all so much. He would sometimes surprise me by picking me up from school, as I usually walked alone. He would also surprise me by giving me sweets and bringing me gifts.

I remember going on lots of long walks with him and sitting on his shoulders or holding onto his jacket when I was tired. I remember one time when my dad took me to the shops on his bike. We went to the off-licence. He would buy me a lucky bag with lots of different things in it while he would go and get his drink.

He would usually buy a bottle of cider, drink it, and fill it up with water. He would then return it and say he bought the wrong one. He would do this many times. Afterwards, we would usually either go to the chip shop or sit in the park on the way back.

My mother stayed at home with my four siblings while my father worked as a supervisor for the Mars chocolate factory until he lost his job. We lived in a three-bedroom house, and when my dad lost his job, we had our electricity turned off, as he could not pay the bill. We never had much, as I remember, but we had a burning fire and candles for light. My brother passed a long cable from our house to my nan's next door so we could still watch TV while having no electricity of our own.

I loved my nan very much. I remember always talking to her through her window when she was washing up, and I used to go round there to see my uncle Jimmy. He would push us on a tree swing that was made for us in our garden, and then my brother and I would climb trees and play in the long grass in the field at the bottom. We would use the cut grass to make an igloo. We also used to go over to the allotments and pick apples from the trees belonging to a man who caught us one day. The man was shouting at my brother, so I ran home.

One day, we were at the back of the garden, and my brother was making a fence because we didn't have one. I remember being on my rocking horse and saying how rubbish it looked. My brother hit me in my face many times. I was screaming, but he would not stop.

My mum must have heard me screaming and came out to find him still hitting me. I told her what had happened while holding my eyes and screaming. Mum put a wet cloth over my eyes and couldn't believe what he had done. My brother was 7 years old at the time and I was 8. When my dad came back, he couldn't believe what my brother had done and beat him for it.

We didn't have much money, but my parents tried to make a nice Christmas for us. I remember getting a silver necklace with a green jade elephant on it. It was my favourite thing from my mother. I also got colouring things, paper, and colouring books, and I often drew pictures for my dad. I wanted to show him how good I was, and sometimes I would joke around with him.

One time, I gave him an aniseed ball. He said he didn't want it, but I told him it was a soft sweet, so he ate it and nearly broke his teeth. I laughed, and then he laughed. He would always call me his little princess. I would go everywhere with him. It was just the two of us; I liked that, especially when I went on his bike with him to the shops. He would buy me sweets, and fruits one time. I remember him buying me a pomegranate; I had to pick out the seeds to eat it.

In the mornings when my mum was cooking breakfast, my dad would sit and drink his coffee and always save me some. My mother would argue with my father about taking my side, when me and my brother were getting into trouble, but I remember my mother always taking my brother's side.

I remember a time when my mother was brushing my teeth. The toothpaste was so strong that I was screaming about it burning my mouth. My mother could be so rough, especially when brushing my hair before I went to school. I never wanted to go to school. And she always forced me to wear dresses I didn't like.

I remember holding on to the banister, trying to stop her pulling me. I used to chew my hair at school. I had thoughts in my head and was nervous and unsure of what I was supposed to do. I could not concentrate or retain anything; I was always worried. I used to just copy my friend's work because it was easier.

* * *

One day, my mum was cooking porridge on a gas cylinder in the kitchen for my brother and me. As she looked out the window, she said out loud to herself, "I wish I could set light to that pile of rubbish at the end of the garden."

The garden was full of bags filled with old clothes and other rubbish. Later on that day, my 8-year-old brother took a lighter and set fire to it all—but he set light to the whole garden too. The firefighters had to be called, and when they arrived, they managed to put it out. I remember them squirting water at all the children who were watching from afar. It was funny.

My mother often looked out the window waiting for my father to come home at night. When he didn't come home and she didn't have money to feed us, they would argue. I remember my mother telling us scary stories and not wanting to be with her at times. She would put me in the cupboard under the stairs to scare me.

Sometimes police would bang down the doors looking for my father. When he would hide, I would try to hide too. I remember not sleeping because I didn't like the dark and always had to have the curtains open so I could see the light from outside. I liked to have my bedroom door open too. One night, I came downstairs after hearing a lot of noise and saw my uncle handcuffed to a chair with a briefcase full of drugs. The police were shouting at my parents to get me up the stairs.

Sometimes, when we had electricity, I would stay awake for hours staring at the light. One time I saw a figure with a long knife like the one I had seen in pictures of the olden days of a man cutting the grass; it looked like my uncle Jimmy. I also saw owls at the bottom of my bed, and one night I felt somebody touching my back going round and round, but my back was against the wall. I felt really scared, so I ran to my mum's room and slept on the floor. I often had bad dreams.

Sometimes we would spend our mornings in our bedrooms. My uncle Melvin rented one of the rooms. I was so bored waiting for my parents to get up one morning, and I remember thinking that I didn't belong in this family. At times, I daydreamed that I was adopted into the family— that my mum and dad were not my real parents.

When we weren't allowed downstairs, my brother and I would play games. We used to knock on my uncle's bedroom door and then run and hide. I also used to make up and tell my brother stories about the hot dog man when he used to annoy me. I would say there was a giant hot dog underneath the floorboards, and if he was bad to me, the hot dog would come out and get him. My brother just laughed and said, "Well, I'll just eat him!"

I said, "You can't, because he is metal!"

He would then believe me and stop annoying me.

Sometimes my brother and I would get along and play together. We would play with his army plastic soldiers, English against the Germans, and then throw marbles to bomb each other. It was fun.

One day, my dad was in a bad mood. He was trying to get something out of the attic—I think it was drugs now, looking back. He couldn't find them, so when my uncle Melvin told him that we were knocking on his door that morning, he took his bad mood out on us.

When me and my brother were getting hit, I would be very scared of Dad, as I thought he might kill me. So I ran downstairs and hid behind my mum, crying because Dad was running after me, shouting that he was going to hit me again. I had never seen him so angry.

* * *

I remember being so depressed sometimes. One night, after Christmas, we watched *Spider-Man* before we went to bed, and my dad carried me upstairs because I had fallen asleep downstairs, which I often did. That night, I dreamt that my uncle was killing me and taking me into the fire next door. He was dragging me down the stairs.

The strange thing was, it wasn't a dream. He *was* trying to save me. There was a big fire in our house, and I was the last person to get out. We nearly died.

The fire had started with a candle falling down the back of the TV. The youngest three were down in the living room while my mum was next door. When she came back and found the fire, my uncle Jimmy came in and saved them, then came to get my brother and me from upstairs. He burned himself on the way out. I remember seeing a vision of a burnt light switch before the fire happened.

Luckily, that day, none of us was hurt, but we were rushed to the hospital to be checked. This was around 1982. We were in the newspapers; I kept the cutting. My mother lost what little she did have—most importantly, her photographs. They were all she wanted. She managed to find a few that were half-burnt.

We moved to a hostel after that, and it was actually okay. It was pleasant, nice, and clean, and we had electricity. We had bunk beds to share, and my mum and dad a double bed. We had a kitchen on one side and a sofa. I remember sitting on my bed and teaching my brothers about Adam and Eve, and talking about the things I remembered from school.

My father went back to see what was left of our house. All my siblings' Christmas presents got burned—apart from mine, because they were upstairs in my bedroom. Theirs were downstairs, as I remember. I had a yellow case with a typewriter and some paper, envelopes, and a telephone inside. I remember my father telling us that my brother went to look in the oven to see if there was a burger still inside. I laughed.

I remember making lots of friends where we lived. I remember me, my sister, and our friends making a pop band, and I sang "Shoot That Poison Arrow." I remember some nice neighbours inviting us in and having drinks and chocolate biscuits.

While we lived in the hostel, my brother kept getting into trouble. One day, the warden knocked on our door because my brother had made a huge dent in the roof of the warden's car. He had jumped up and down on it. My dad was so mad I thought he was going to kill my brother.

I remember us moving to another house similar to the one we lived in before but just around the corner. I liked the new house because it was near my cousins, so we used to cut through our neighbours' and we were there. We had a huge six-foot Christmas tree in the middle of our garden and lots of roses.

I had my own bedroom in the new house and my brothers too. My parents shared with the three younger siblings. My mum tried to make it nice for us.

I remember there were always people coming in and out of our home. We always had somebody staying over on the sofa, and we had lots of parties. One time I came down and saw my mother with lots of people on the floor everywhere. They were all drunk. I saw my mother sniffing white powder up her nose from a mirror. There was lots of money on the floor and alcoholic drinks everywhere—and lots of ice lollies in the freezer that I was told I wasn't allowed to have because they were alcoholic.

The next day, I saw my mother baking, cleaning, doing washing, and doing all the things a mother should be doing. I remember watching her baking a cake and an apple pie.

I remember my father used to take me to school. I loved that school. I had such lovely teachers there. I would often win competitions for my artwork, and one time when I was seven or eight, I did a road-safety painting and won a certificate from the Lord Mayor of London. My painting was hung in the gallery.

I had the same teachers as my father had when he was at school. I remember them teaching us the Bible, about

Jesus Christ, and about how we could pray to Him if we needed something. We were saying the Lord's Prayer, and I remember when they told me stories, I would be asking them questions. I was very interested in the idea that if I needed something, I could pray to Jesus.

One day, it was snowing, and I was walking to school by myself. I must have been about 8 or 9 by this time. It was really slippery, and I remember holding onto the fence, wondering how I was going to get to school and praying to God to help me, when a dog knocked me down. I couldn't get up—it was so slippery. But suddenly, a lorry driver stopped and started shouting at the dog to get off me. He held my hand and walked me all the way to school.

I remember that when I got there, the teachers came out to get me. I was worried because I had a big splinter in my hand that my mother had told me would go septic if she couldn't get it out—which she had tried to do, but I didn't let her touch me. She told me I would have to have my hand chopped off.

My mother also told me that when I was 2 years old, she slapped me round the face because I was happy and laughing. I don't know why she told me that. She often told me that I reminded her of my dad. I thought to myself, *Maybe she told me that because she felt guilty.*

Anyway, I was upset about the splinter, so my Headmaster who was also our teacher for the day, took it out of my hand. He was so nice to me. All of my teachers were. One even paid for me to go on a school holiday. I had never been on holiday before, so I was excited. I had so much fun. I was the only one on that school holiday who couldn't ride a bike, because I'd never had one. The teachers took the time to teach me, and I loved it.

When I got back, I wished I had never gone on holiday. I was so happy until I got home, and then I was so upset, depressed, and crying. I didn't know how to stop the tears from running down my face. It was because I'd had such a nice time, and then coming back was horrible. I remember my mum asking me why I was crying and telling me to stop, but I couldn't.

My mum was waiting for my father to come home, I heard from somebody that he was selling drugs. I remember nights waking up with my mother coming into my room, screaming and shouting and sitting on my bed with my youngest brother in her arms holding a knife because she was scared of my dad. I remember not been able to get to sleep, as my dad always used to hide his drugs in my wardrobe and lock it, and in the middle of the night, he would go in the wardrobe to get it out again.

One day, my mother was locked out of the house by my dad, and she threw stones at the window to wake me up. I had to sneak downstairs, open the door, and let her in. She was scared of my dad. Most nights, they would be fighting and screaming. I would put my hands over my ears and tense my body up in fear.

I remember that many times, we went to a women's aid refuge. My mum would get up in the middle of the night and get us ready. We would be standing at the telephone box until somebody came to pick us up. That happened many times, but she would still go back to him.

One time we were in a bed and breakfast. My mum took me to school and told me I had to walk back by myself. I had anxiety all day at school worrying that something was going to happen to me on the way home. I ran until I came to a main road. I was waiting there for a long time, getting anxious and worried that I was going to forget my way home. Eventually, I just ran across the road and got hit by a car. The next thing I knew, I was in the hospital screaming.

I stayed in hospital for a few days; luckily, I only had minor injuries. My mother came and brought me some nice things, and my teachers came to see me. My dad came to visit, and they got back together again. It was fine for a while, and then they were back to arguing and fighting once more.

Chapter 2

One day, my mother left with the lodger who was staying at our house. I remember that day because she bought us some sweets and drinks and left us with my uncle Jimmy. I love Jimmy; he was my favourite uncle. I remember my cousin coming round and staying with us, and I remember my cousins wanting to play with my dolls but I wouldn't let them. My uncle told me to share, but I was crying a lot because I didn't want them to, so he took the dolls from me and let my cousins have them.

The same night, I was told I sleepwalked downstairs with my pillow, taking an ornament from the mantelpiece and placing it on my pillow. I remember at the time I was so sad. I was missing my mother, crying every night, praying for her to come back. It was the worst pain I've ever felt. I remember being closer to God than ever at this point, feeling His love for me.

I was stuck with my father, who was never there and had strangers in the house all the time. I felt responsible for my three brothers and one sister; then my nan took my sister, so I was responsible for the others. I remember having to cook and clean and take my brothers to school before I went to school because I was the oldest. I remember my dad hitting my 4-year-old brother for wetting the bed. I screamed at him to stop, saying, "It's because of you he is wetting the bed!" Then Dad stopped.

I remember my older brother digging big holes in the garden making traps one day. He knew my dad used to cut across the garden, so when Dad ran across the next time, he fell into the hole. My brother had put a fork inside it, so my dad hurt his foot, and he was so mad. He went to hit my brother, but my brother climbed the big tree in the garden so Dad couldn't get hold of him.

I remember many times going across the garden to my cousins' house and staying there because I didn't want to go back home. One day, I was with my cousins, and we went back to my home and saw people there. There were two people in the bathroom with needles, so my cousin went and told her mum, My dad had a go at me wanting to know who I had told. I told him it was just my cousin.

My mum tried to get custody of us kids after six months of not seeing us. My dad asked for my opinion on things to get for Christmas, and he used to bring me gifts home, usually gold earrings or necklaces or some sort of jewellery. My dad's friend kept on at us to choose our dad over our mum. I didn't want to choose.

They fought in court over us, and my mother won custody. We had to move to Oxford in 1985. We saw my dad every other weekend until it stopped. My dad had lost the house and he became homeless, so we lost touch with him.

* * *

We lived in a women's refuge. It was very friendly. We made lots of friends, and there were lots of children there. I liked it. I remember it was near Christmastime, me and the other children made up a play and performed it for us, and I went shopping for Christmas presents. My mum found a Michael Jackson doll for me; I used to love his music, and he was my favourite singer at the time. I remember my dad got me a Walkman. It was the last Christmas I had with my dad that I can remember.

My mum met someone in Oxford, and she had another baby. By this time, I had four brothers and one sister. My mum was much happier and made lots of friends there, but she started drinking a lot with her friends. I liked it there because everybody looked after everybody and helped each other with the children. They also took turns to cooking dinner for each other.

We moved to a five-bedroom house in Oxford, and I was allowed to choose my own room. I had pink flowers on the wallpaper and two windows, one at the side and one at the front. There was also a built-in cupboard. It was always really cold in my room.

At times, I remember Mum's friend Jackie coming round with her family and staying for the holidays. She and Mum would be drinking a lot and going out, saying that I would be fine watching all of the children. I was cooking dinner and cleaning up all the time.

I used to like it when my nan would come and stay with us sometimes, and at Christmastime. Mum would be in a bad mood before Nan came because she didn't really want Nan to stay, but I liked it because Mum used to be a better mum when Nan came down. My nan would spend time with us, talking to us about the olden days and just listening to us. I learned a lot from her. She always taught us to be well-mannered and how to take care of ourselves.

Mum's boyfriend, my younger brother's father, would come and stay sometimes, but they would always end up arguing, and he would leave and then come back. I didn't really like him because he was so stupid at times. At other times, I felt sorry for him, because my mother was not very nice to him.

One time, when I came in and saw that the hamsters were gone, I said, "Where are the hamsters?"

Mum told me they ate her tablecloth, so she threw them to the cat. I told her she was evil, and she just laughed—but I know she felt bad from her expression. She carried on drinking more and more each day and evening, even if we only had the bare minimum to live on.

We needed many things and had to go without food, clothes, etc. When she went shopping, she would hide drink in a bottle when she was out and about. When she didn't have money for drink, she became abusive and insulting. She used to put me down so many times, telling me I was stupid and many other things.

I would always try to make her happy and do nice things for her so she could be happy and be in a good mood. I would do what she wanted me to do, even if I was tired of cleaning and looking after the children. But still she was nasty and told me she just didn't want to look at my face.

One time, she made me really upset. Then she tried to hug me and tell me she was sorry for everything. I didn't want her near me, because she had never done that ever, since I was very young.

* * *

I remember when I was around the age of 13 or 14 years, it was the holidays, and my mum decided to take us to stay with her friend Jackie and their family. I didn't know we were about to stay there for the next four weeks. I remember sharing a bed with my friend and my brothers sharing a room with her brother and sister. I remember long days staying confined in the room all day and all night, not having anything to do other than playing cards or a board game. The boys had a TV in their room, which kept them amused.

My mum and her friend Jackie, along with Jackie's bloke, would be downstairs drinking, night after night and day after day. They only had the little ones downstairs. We had to stay upstairs, between the two rooms, eating, sleeping, and entertaining each other. We hardly ever went outside and weren't allowed to make any noise either. It was as though we were in a prison.

If we made the slightest noise, my mother's friend's bloke would come running up the stairs, threatening us that we would be staying longer in the rooms for the noise we made. I don't think it made any difference if we were quiet. He used to spend a lot of time listening to us outside the door. He gave me the creeps. He used to say inappropriate things to us, especially me and my friend.

We were together most of the time. Sometimes we would argue, which resulted in me and my friend getting split up. I would be told to go in her brother's room, and the other children would be told to go in with her. I didn't mind, because I got a chance to watch my television programme, which I really liked. I also got along with her brother really well. It was a change in every boring day we spent together.

My friend's brother was fixing his computer, but we liked watching the same television programme. I remember Jackie's bloke outside the door making remarks regarding me and my friend's brother, which was stupid, because I never thought of him in that way. Besides, I had a boyfriend.

We would sometimes go to the park or to the shop to get groceries on the odd occasion. We had a little change that we were allowed to spend. I would get some treats to share with the others; being stuck in the room, we would have minimal things to eat. We were hungry while my mum and her friend would spend all their money on alcohol every day partying. I felt like we were never going to leave this prison.

One day, as I was on the way to the shops and to the park, my mum wanted me to take my younger brother with me. We played at the park for a while, and while we were playing, I looked up to find this boy staring at me and asking questions about who I was. When my friend would come along with my brothers, he would start teasing me. I remember one time he said something to me and it caused a fight between him and my brother, who beat the boy up.

It was nearly Christmas, and usually we would have good Christmases with my mum, but this year was not good. I spent Christmas upstairs with just my brothers, my friend, and her sister and brother. We hardly saw my mother in those weeks. We were only allowed to come down to cook or clean up, along with going to the shop.

I remember getting one small gift, while the others got a few. One small little make-up box. It was not Christmas for me or for my brothers. I remember dreaming, as I tended to do to get out of this negative feeling of despair. I dreamt I was somewhere else, and when I woke up, it was Christmas.

There was lots of food and family, and everybody was happy. We had many presents all around. Then I woke up for real and saw that it was a dream, which was very disappointing. I just wanted to go back to sleep and get back to the dream.

I remember arguing with my friend; I don't know what it was about, but sometimes she could be so nasty. I remember being split up and put in another room, on my own. It was even more boring to have no one to talk to, as I was isolated even more.

I remember staring at the window and then proceeding to look round for something to do. I remember looking at her things and jewellery on the side. I remember touching it but I never remember taking it. Not long after that, somebody noticed it was missing and searched all my things, knowing that I was in the room, but I still don't remember taking it. It was somehow found in the pocket of my jacket. I'd never done something like this before, and I still don't believe I did it. It was the first time I'd seen my mother in weeks, and she hit me for taking it.

I remember my mum and Jackie going out shopping in the daytime, always out and never around. I was never allowed downstairs apart from Jackie's bloke always telling us off. I remember he would spend hours with my friend's youngest sister in the bathroom. We didn't know what was going on. I remember my friend telling me he was doing something to her; it made sense as to the way he was with us and the way he would be hanging around us all.

I didn't feel comfortable with him around. I hated him. It was like the feeling of being in hell, and I felt like I've been there many times. I just wanted to run away.

Finally, I remember my mum's boyfriend coming up

and saying that he didn't mind taking a few of us home. I jumped at the chance to go back. I offered to do the cleaning. I tried everything just to get out of there.

I was allowed to go back with my brother, which was such a nice feeling. I don't know if I could ever forgive my mother for doing this to us, and I try not to think about it most of the time because there's no point. Eventually, my mother and the rest of the children came home too.

We had missed so much school. My friends didn't think I was ever going to come back, and my boyfriend was so happy to see me. I was so surprised to see how many gifts I had from him. I was very happy to feel the love from my friends.

Each gift my boyfriend gave me was wrapped in lots of gold paper, and when it was opened, gold pieces flew all over the place. It was so thoughtful. The way he wrapped each present surprised me and made me feel so happy. When I took the presents home to show my mother, she liked them because there was lots of make-up and perfume, so I decided to give them to her. I just wanted her to be happy.

The week after that, she told me that my boyfriend came round and posted a gold necklace. She then showed it to me; she had that also. She would be nice to me for a little while, but even if I didn't give it to her, she would just take it anyway. She would sell it to buy more drinks. She would drink two litres of vodka a day when she could afford it.

Chapter 3

When I was nearly 16, I used to do a babysitting job. It was good because I used to earn some money for myself. Sometimes me and my sister would do it together. The people we babysat for would come back early and say we could stay if we wanted, and sometimes there would be another person there who would always chat to me, telling me nice things, which made me feel good about myself. He tried to get closer to me and tried to persuade me to be with him. It was late and he tried again and wanted me to stay, but my sister came banging on the door.

When I didn't come home with my sister, my Mum was really angry and came round banging on the door to fetch me home. She knew there was something going on, so she was in a bad mood. I remember waiting at the back of the garden until she went to bed before sneaking in.

On my birthday when I turned 16, my mother bought me a birthday card. I was happy until I read it. She thought she was being funny by putting German signs instead of kisses in it, but it was very hurtful.

When I left school, my mother told me I had one day to

get a job, otherwise I would be thrown out of the house. I think she just wanted more money or me out of the way. To my surprise, I did find a job in a hotel serving and cooking breakfast. I was a bit nervous, but I'd had a lot of practical experience, so I did well. The only problem was, I had to memorise all the orders. But I had a way of remembering, because I didn't want anybody to know I couldn't read or write. I knew from experience that people looked at you differently, and I wasn't stupid.

I gave my mother most of the money, as I had to. With what was left, I would buy myself some things. In my spare time, I would babysit for some other people whom I became friends with. They would take me out with them and try to pair me up with somebody, which I wasn't really interested in.

One time I met somebody in a pub whom I liked. He was twice my age and very confident. I started going on dates with him. He would drive up just down the road from our house to fetch me, I would tell my mother I was going out to meet a friend. She would tell me I had to be back by 10 p.m., so we used to go to a club or a pub. He would buy me drinks to get me drunk and then try to get close to me, but all I really wanted was to be loved and cared for. I wasn't interested in anything else.

I would come back home, and my mum just knew I had been with somebody. I don't know how she knew, but she did, and she would go mad. She would be drunk and would drag me by my hair and hit me over and over. She did this many times, but it didn't stop me. I couldn't stop seeing him.

One time, she went crazy; I thought I was going to die.

She smashed up my room, and I just wanted to throw myself out the window. I couldn't cope anymore. She was like a mad person. My brother had to come in to stop her because I was screaming. She had covered my arms with bruises, I was so scared I ran out of the house and went to the person I babysat for. When I got there, she phoned the police and social services.

I stayed with them for a little while. I was really ill. My mother and her friend came banging on their door, demanded I go home, and threatened them. Social services put me into a children's home, and I stayed there for a while. I didn't want to go, but I didn't have a choice. I felt embarrassed and ashamed. I had scratches on my face and looked a mess.

A friend of mine went and collected some of my clothes and things. She brought them to me, but when I opened the bag, I saw that my mother had cut them all up. I was really upset, because I had bought them with my own money. It upset me so much, thinking, *How could she do that to me?*

* * *

A few weeks later, it was nearly Easter, and I wanted to see my brothers and give them Easter eggs. My mother was still angry, but she came around. I just wanted to make it up and see my brothers. We started to get on again, but she found out that the man I was seeing was married. I told her I didn't know; he told me he was separated. My mother wanted to kill him.

Then I found I was pregnant, so she didn't want me to have anything to do with him anymore. She wanted me to keep the baby but have nothing to do with him, but I couldn't do that, so it caused so many problems. He didn't want to see me for a while when he found out I was pregnant, then he came around. He told me that he was separated and that they were going for a divorce. We started seeing each other again.

The home workers took me to the doctor. Lots of people were suggesting I have an abortion because I was only 16, apart from one doctor who was happy for me. I didn't want to have an abortion; I was happy to have a baby. The father was happy too but was still living with his ex-wife and his four boys.

I soon moved out of the children's home and had a room, my own place. I worked up until I was seven and a half months pregnant. The place where I was staying helped me to get a grant to buy baby things.

While I was still living there, somebody got into my room, and certain things went missing—food and other small things—and the curtains had fallen down. I worked it out and realised the person next door to me must have tried to get through my window from the balcony.

I told the lady who was working there. She checked the room of the person next to me and found the missing things. The people who were staying there, who I had befriended by making food and drinks for them and chatting with them, had gone through my window and stolen from me.

The worker confronted my neighbour. I wouldn't have minded sharing anything if he had needed it or if he was hungry. I would've helped him and given him what I had, but I didn't like the fact that someone had sneaked into my room and gone through my things.

Soon after that, I moved to a mother-and-baby flat that

was brand-new, and I loved it. I started to buy things bit by bit. I also got a grant to furnish it. I was still working at the time. My partner would come round more and more, excited for me to have a baby girl. Hopefully, I would start to put things together. But then I had contractions.

My friend from the children's home moved in at around the same time, and we were in the same block of flats. She was downstairs and I was up. She was also pregnant; she had a baby boy and me a baby girl. She was there when I gave birth.

I never thought I would feel the way I did. I had this overwhelming feeling of love for my baby and being responsible for somebody. I couldn't believe how amazing I felt even after all the pain and how tired I was. I just couldn't go to sleep. I kept on staring at this baby.

She had a few complications when she was born, so they had to suck out all the stuff she ate inside me. I was overdue by two weeks; the doctor delivered her, and lots of medical people came into the room. I had to have stitches and was sick a lot before giving birth.

My mother came to visit me. She'd had a baby boy three months earlier, so I had a brother three months older than my daughter. I now had six brothers and one sister.

My partner came round about the same time my mother was there, and she said things like, "She doesn't look like you. She doesn't look anything like you," which was wrong because she *did*. He was a bit off with me and went home and looked at some pictures of his babies. I was told she looked the same as his sons did when they were born. My mother was just being nasty.

I went to stay with my mother for two weeks because

she knew a lot about babies and children; she was very good with babies and gave good advice at times. She helped me a lot. She had also wanted another daughter, so she loved to help look after mine.

* * *

Once I had moved back to the flat for a few months, my mum would come round and visit us, and she made friends with my friend downstairs. She encouraged my friend and I to go out with her to a nightclub and encouraged us to drink vodka before we went out so that by the time we got there, we were already drunk. I was so drunk and out of control I didn't even realise I was falling all over the place.

One guy on the doors tried it on with me. I tried to get out and eventually I opened the fire door and left. I never wanted to feel like that again. When Mum asked me to go out with her again, I told her I didn't want to because of my experience. I didn't like it at all, so she used to take my friend instead.

One day, when my mother was in my friend's flat and I was looking after my baby, I saw my friend sniffing gas with my mum. She was sitting there, and the baby was lying on the couch. I was shocked. I said to my mother, "How could you let her do that?"

She was so mad. I walked out and went upstairs, but she followed me and hit me in my face. She also took the TV that she had leant me. I didn't speak to her for a long time. It was so hurtful that she had gone down to see my friend and her baby and not once asked about me or been up to see her own granddaughter. My friend would tell me that my mother was saying bad things, private things about me to her. I was so upset about that.

One time my friend said she was just going to pop out to the shop and gave me the baby monitors so I could hear if he was crying downstairs till she got back. I was in at the time, so I said okay, thinking that she was only going to be ten minutes. In the early hours of the morning, I heard a baby crying and thought it was strange, so I went downstairs to see. There was nobody there, so I took him out of his cot and brought him upstairs and put him in my daughter's cot, putting my daughter in my bed.

When my friend eventually came back, she was shocked to see he wasn't there and came upstairs banging on my door. She was shouting, "Where is he?"

I wanted to teach her a lesson, so I said, "What do you mean?" I pretended I didn't know what she was talking about.

She said, "Somebody took him!"

I said, "What do you mean? Where is he?"

She eventually admitted to me that she had been to a nightclub, so I told her that I had him and she was mad at me. I was in bed ill at the time, so I just wanted get rid of her. She was still shouting at me the next day, so I had it out with her.

I was so annoyed with her. She wasn't a very good mother, but I had tried to encourage her to be better. I showed her how I did things, because she didn't have any idea, and her son was always ill. She knew nothing about how to bring up a baby, not even how to change the steriliser or wash the bottles properly. She was just tipping the milk out and putting them straight in the steriliser. One day, she left the baby with my mother for weeks while she just went off with her friend on holiday without even notifying my mother.

* * *

After a while, my mother and I were talking again, and she came round to have a few drinks with my partner. One time, she made a pass at him in front of me. Another time, my partner would get drunk and embarrass me in front of my friend I had invited round. He also insulted her and was very nasty.

I got so badly depressed I just wanted to kill myself. I took lots of tablets, which was stupid, I know. It especially hurt when my partner would drink and make passes at my friends to get me jealous. He often wanted to take me out to a pub, wanting me to dress up. When he wasn't drinking, he was good to me, and a good father. He used to fix things for us and knew how to cook and always did the cooking when he wasn't drinking.

If I would go out with him, he would be very happy, but he would get very jealous. I started to realise that I didn't like going out with him when he drank, because he would get more drunk and aggressive. I didn't even want to be around him, because he just started on me for any reason. If a man looked at me, he would accuse me of things.

He started fights with other people sometimes. I had to look at the floor all night, otherwise he would hit me on the way back from the pub or when we got back home. He would go on and on about what I had done wrong when I hadn't done anything wrong at all; it was all in his head.

In the morning he would apologise and say he didn't know what he was doing.

I started to go back to college couple of days a week to do English and maths lessons, which I didn't finish at school because I had a lot of time off during my childhood. I wanted to read to my daughter, and I wanted better for her. I used to get so frustrated trying to read a book and having to sound out the words. The good thing was, she learnt to read at a very early age She was very clever. She was learning at the same time I was.

My partner got so jealous. He didn't like me going to college. He would always try to upset me before I went. He would cause an argument on my way out the door so I couldn't go because I was too upset.

I didn't want to be with him, so I told him I was going to stay at my mother's, like I usually did when he did that. I had always forgiven him, thinking that he couldn't help it, and begged him not to drink. But he started to get worse and worse. It got to the point where I didn't want to go anywhere near him. He used to try to force me to sleep with him, but I wouldn't, so he would hit me or break things in the home because he knew I tried to keep it nice.

He blackmailed me and started burning the carpet with a cigarette. He would do this in front of my 2-year-old daughter, which resulted in her copying him. I'd just had enough. I didn't want him in my life anymore, so I stayed at my mother's for a few weeks. He refused to move out, so I had to go to a lawyer and get an injunction against him to try to get him out of my flat. I would stay at my mum's or my friend's house, but eventually, I had to go back.

He used to hide in cupboards and scare me by jumping

out. He used to listen to me talking on the phone to see if I had anybody else, when I didn't want anybody else. He would follow me when I went to my friends and used to question me for ages. Why was I five minutes late? He was so possessive.

I couldn't even go to the bathroom. If I locked it, he would break the door down. He would ask me over and over again what I was doing and where I'd been. I couldn't cope with it, so I just lost it. I started shouting, and I threw the coffee table over. People used to tell me that he was following me. We would start arguing when we were at home, and he would pick on me for the tiniest thing I did wrong.

I was pregnant at the time with our second child. One night, he came back drunk, and I pretended to be asleep. I was sleeping in my daughter's bed with her. He kicked me in the back, to wake me up. My neighbour below heard me screaming and phoned the police. They took him away, but when he came back again, he blackmailed me and took a hammer to the baby's buggy.

After that, I went to court and got an injunction. He broke that and took my daughter out of the nursery and ran off with her. He got arrested and was warned not to go anywhere near me. Not long afterwards, I moved to a two-bedroom house, where I had his second baby. I was very depressed at the time, and when I bumped into him again several times, I wanted him to see the baby. He was really nice to me and started giving me money and running to see the children.

Eventually, I had him back again, because he told me he had changed. He was nice for maybe a week or so, but then I started to see a difference in him again. He would be impatient with the baby because she would cry a lot and started drinking again.

One day, he came back drunk and came towards me wanting to sleep with me, but I refused. I told him, "You've been drinking."

He just lost it, so I told him to get out. He threatened to wake the baby up and break things. He started shouting and threatened to wake up my older daughter, who was 3 at the time. I didn't want him to do that, so I just gave in to him. I felt rubbish.

One time, he was frustrated and threw the baby on the bed because she was sick on him. He was still drinking. He was cooking and taking something out of the oven when he kicked the bike and it hit my daughter's head. This time he knew I would never get back with him, but he kept on saying it was an accident. I didn't care, I went to my mother's where my brother stayed. My brother waited for him and beat him up, telling him to stay away from me, but he wouldn't. So my brother stayed with me at my home for a while, but eventually he had to go back home.

Even though I prayed to God to keep this man away, he came back again that night. He was drunk as usual. I just knew something was going to happen. He had a key, so I couldn't even lock the door. I only had the latch, and he broke that off.

He started to blackmail me again and took electrical parts from each electrical item in my house so that they wouldn't work. He knew how to fix things and take things apart, but I couldn't. When I went shopping, I couldn't put food in the freezer. Eventually he did put some of the parts back, but not the TV, washing machine, or radio. I didn't care. I just wanted him gone.

He threatened to kill me and do to me what my brother did to him. If he couldn't have me, no one was going to be with me. At this point, I didn't want anybody. He would try to push himself up against me, but I would push him away because I was disgusted. He kept on trying and trying, so I just lost it and kicked him. I couldn't believe myself and what I did.

Then he tried to strangle me. He was ripping my hair out and stomping the keys in my head. I thought I was going to die. He put his hand firmly around my mouth until I couldn't breathe, but I finally managed to get away from him and went to my daughter's room. I don't know how, but I did. The neighbours once again had heard me, saw me through the window, and called the police.

He refused to open the door to the police. They wanted to see me from the window and asked me if I was alright. I was so scared. I told them I was, but I nodded my head no so they could see I wasn't. They started to smash down the door because he wouldn't open it, but he eventually did, so he was arrested. I had to go to the police station to be photographed. He was imprisoned, but when he got out he started phone-calling me twenty to thirty times a day. I had to be wired up to a police recorder so they could record him threatening me.

So many times, he would tell me what I was doing. He would hide at the back of my garden and ask me why I was looking in the cupboards. He could see me. I was so scared. I was more scared not being with him than being with him. He knew things that I did in the day that I didn't understand. It did seem weird, but I would check the cupboards just to make sure he wasn't hiding in them.

I would have detectives on one occasion following me when he tried to take my daughter out of school and threatened to kill me while on one occasion when I was going shopping. I had detectives following me to catch him, and he eventually went to prison. I was so relieved, even though it was hard for me. I had to go to the Laundrette to wash my clothes, and my neighbour leant me a TV, but I was happy for the first time in a long time. I felt at peace again.

When he got out again, he would stalk me. One time, he tried being nice by giving me a gold ring and forcing it on my finger. I just wanted to avoid him, so I just went on my way back from going out to see my friend because she had just had a baby. He must've known what time I was coming back, because he was waiting in the alleyway and tried to force himself on me. Again, I thought he was going to kill me because he was so angry and I was trying to get away.

Eventually, I found a house and I ran to bang on the door. When the people came out, they scared him away. The police came and took a statement, and he had to go to Crown Court for indecent assault. I had to testify. It was horrible seeing him staring at me. Thankfully, he served another eighteen to twenty-four months.

Chapter 4

For a while after that, I was on my own, but I eventually met somebody else. Although I wasn't interested in another relationship, he kept on asking me to go out with him. I wasn't sure, as he was related to my brother's girlfriend. I didn't want another relationship with anybody at that time, but eventually we all went out together.

He told me he had split up from his wife after doing something he regretted, and that he was sorry for what he had done. He seemed honest and nice enough, so I trusted him. We got on really well. We would talk for hours and went out places together. He was very generous.

Later I found out that he had been diagnosed with manic depression. He was generally really good, but sometimes he wouldn't take his tablets, and I would see the evil side of him. One minute he would be giving me a few hundred pounds to go shopping and buy some new clothes, the next minute he would change, cutting everything up. One time, my youngest daughter came in, and he had cut all of her hair off when I was at a friend's house wrapping Christmas presents. It was unforgivable.

We would split up, and he would go off and have affairs with other women, then beg me to have him back. Like a fool, I would. He started to disagree with lots of things and became controlling over everything I did. He would ask me to do things I really didn't want to do and blackmail me if I didn't, but I refused anyway. He became abusive and hit me, and then we would split up.

He would follow me and be really nice, asking me if I wanted a lift and if we could just be friends because we were like a family, so I agreed because I had the children with me and it was raining. He would then blackmail me again and take me down a one-way street with my kids in the back and turn off all the lights and wait for the next car to go into us so I would agree.

Once I got home, I tried to phone the police, but he put a knife to my throat and threatened to kill me. One minute, he was being nice, the next minute, he was threatening to kill me—and then the next minute, hr was asking me to marry him. He was crazy.

I had never been so scared, so I told him I would think about it. He went, so I locked the door and then phoned the police. I just had to get rid of him. He scared me because he was so unpredictable.

After we had been apart for a while, we happened to bump into one another, which was awkward. He remained nice until one time he saw me talking to a friend and just came in amongst us and hit my friend because he was so jealous. We weren't together; there was nothing in it. I'd just met an old friend from school and had coffee with him.

Then he would cry and tell me how much he loved me, bring me flowers, and do really nice things for me. One time he went and found my father and brought him to me, which was amazing. I was pleased to see him. Finally he saw his grandchildren and said how beautiful they were and how proud he was of me.

I didn't know what to do to help my father, because he had made himself homeless. He stayed with me for a bit, then he went to see my mother and stayed with her for a little while, but he wanted to go back to Slough where we used to live. He was accustomed to living in a certain way, and he just wanted to go back there. He was an alcoholic, on the streets, and occasionally smoked drugs.

I knew my ex-partner had done this to try to win me back, and it was such a lovely thing. But I couldn't get back with him. He was too controlling, and I was scared of him.

I used to work on weekends, and he would look after the girls, although I was uneasy about it. One day, I just had an overwhelming feeling that something was wrong. I rang him on my break and he assured me everything was fine, but I knew when I got home that something wasn't right. He had put my youngest daughter upstairs in her room for hours and just played with my oldest one downstairs. After this unsettling feeling, I stopped him from looking after them.

Another time, I had another job, but he was so jealous he tried to get me pregnant. He put my birth-control pills down the toilet. I had still carried on taking them, because I knew I couldn't trust him. There was something about him. I definitely didn't want a child with him.

One day, he found out I was taking my pills and hit me in my face. After that, I finished with him for good, but he carried on pestering me to get back with him time and time again. Weeks would pass, a couple of months, but he was still pestering me.

My brother started to come round and stay with me sometimes, and his friend too. I would cook dinner for them, and then my brother told me how much his friend liked me. Sometimes the friend would come round by himself, and we would watch a movie together. He was good with the kids, and we had lots of fun together, going out places. The kids loved him and spent a lot of time with him having fun.

He was like a big kid himself, and it actually felt comfortable to be with somebody without feeling scared. I was able to be myself, so I had a lot of fun with him. And finally my ex left me alone because I was with somebody who would stand up to him.

After being with my brother's friend for a short while, I became pregnant. I was happy, because I wanted another baby, and he was really happy, because my brother would come and stay and they would drink together. It was annoying sometimes, because he started drinking a lot like the others. I got stressed being pregnant and having to put up with them both drinking and being silly.

We started to argue a lot. Then he would stop drinking, and everything was fine—but when we had the baby, he was useless. He didn't want to hold her; he was very immature. He had a lot of good points, but we just didn't get on, so I went away for a while. I found out he was having an affair with somebody, so we split up. Then I forgave him, and we got back together.

* * *

At the same time, I met a friend from my school. She had a daughter the same age as mine. She was such a good example to me; she was a lot older than me and gave me good advice. She was almost the same age as my mother, and I respected her a lot as well as her opinion. She looked after my children while I was searching for direction in my life.

My sister-in-law set me up with the Jehovah's Witnesses. I was excited to speak to them, as I'd been searching for something in my life for many years, but when I got there and they started to tell me about the church, I started arguing with them. I didn't believe what they were telling me; it just didn't feel right.

I knew there was a God, but I didn't know what church to join. When I was younger, I visited the Catholic Church, but I didn't like the speakers shouting out repentance. I just said to myself, *God is love; he's not like that.* I wanted to go to church, but I didn't like it there; it didn't feel right to me.

When I got back home and told my friend, she told me everything about her church. What she said I believed in my heart, and I wanted to know more and more of what was making sense to me. I told her, "Let's go to this church." It would have been good for the children to go, so we did, but there was nobody there.

We went again the following week, and the missionaries were there. It took quite a few months, but eventually I was baptised along with my eldest daughter. I was happy. At the time, I wasn't married, so my partner and I had to get married. Obviously, it didn't last long, because he said I had changed. We were just about to get a mortgage together on a house, but I stopped going out with him. He had an affair with the same girl again, and we were finished. I was so sad and depressed for the kids.

* * *

I started to get back on my feet again. Christmas was coming, so I started to decorate the whole house. It was a good Christmas, but shortly after, my Mum died. I went to see her in the hospital one last time after she had been rushed into hospital many times because of her liver.

She had lost over five stone and had been dating somebody before she died, and he had left her. He had got her in a worse state, as she drank more than ever, and then finally she passed away. I was so angry and upset when I saw my brothers. My youngest brother was about 6 or 7, and he was stroking her hair. The doctor told him that she had died, and then he said, "But when is she coming home?" which broke my heart.

They had to live with my sister-in-law. I wanted to take one of my brothers, but it was hard at the time, because I had three daughters and only lived in a two-bedroom house. I tried to move to a bigger place, but I wasn't able to, so my other sister had my younger brother in the end.

The only good thing before my mum died was that when she was in hospital, I came to visit her and often talked to her about the church. She was convinced it was some kind of cult, but in the end I gave her the Book of Mormon, and she actually read it. When I returned, she was asking questions, because I think she wanted to know that she was going somewhere when she died, even though she was an atheist.

I started to get back on my feet again and decided to work as a childminder. I asked my friend how to get started. I did some courses and kept myself busy. I would teach in the church, being a ward missionary.

At that time, I made good friendships with many

different missionaries. They had so much fun with me and the kids. I used to see my mum's drinking friend from time to time; her children grew up with me. She talked about my mum, and she could see a change in me. I talked to her about many things about the church and how it was helping me.

One day, she approached me, wanting to know about the church and wanting to come to chat. I was surprised, as she was the last person I would've thought would be interested. Not long after, she was baptised, along with her son and daughter. It was great. We helped each other. But not long afterward, she had an illness and died, after her daughter had looked after her. Then sadly, her daughter died of cancer too, leaving her son and younger daughter to her sister.

I carried on seeing them for a while; we looked at old photographs. But her oldest daughter didn't believe in the church, and her younger brother stopped going. At this time, a couple of my younger brothers started using drugs, and my oldest brother would drink a lot. I tried to visit one of them to help him, but he would hang around with lots of unsavoury characters, and my mum's house would be full of them.

One day I just lost it because I bought some food round for him and there were a lot of his friends there drinking. I knew a couple of them, and they offered me a drink. I said, "No, I don't drink," so they asked why and I told them. It was so funny, because the whole room went quiet. They started asking me questions, and I answered them, even though at times I didn't know how to. I felt the Holy Ghost confirming to them the truth. One of them actually said, "If I didn't drink, I would go to the church."

A year after my mother died, my dad died. My two brothers and I visited him. I took him some cookies. He was so happy to see us. He looked so skinny. I went to go and see him the next day, but he had died. I was so sad. It was as if he was holding on until we came to visit him. I'm so glad we did.

Chapter 5

I decided to go back to college and do childminding part-time. I also started art and access-into-university courses along with part-time maths and English, which was frustrating at times because of my dyslexia. The access course was good, and I made some friends.

After my mum died, I decided that each year, at Christmastime, we would go abroad to a different country. That was the plan, anyway. The first one was Spain. I brought along one of my brothers. It was so nice—we saw the volcanoes and the whales and the dolphins.

The second trip was to Salt Lake City in America. It was cool. I went through the Temple and stayed with some members of the church. We went to Park City to ski. The family was so nice and friendly.

We went to Brigham Young University. We also went to watch basketball. The kids went to school for the day—the children of the family we were staying with were learning about English culture, so it was a good opportunity. We also went to a concert of the Tabernacle Choir, which was amazing, but we were so tired and jet-lagged we fell asleep halfway through.

We stayed with another family for the second week, during which we had a lovely Christmas. They were so thoughtful and bought presents for all of us. It was so high up in the mountains. One weird thing that happened on that trip: when I took my three daughters to the airport on the way to America, I was asked if they were mine and if I was going to bring them back!

On our third holiday abroad, we decided to go somewhere warm. We went to a travel agent but still weren't sure where to go. The agent told us she had just come back from Egypt and recommended it, and so that was our choice.

When we got to the airport there, it was a bit scary. Soldiers with guns were everywhere, and they were very abrupt. We got to Egypt late and were tired, but the hotel was amazing. We decided to go round the shops. People were so friendly, offering us red tea and talking about the history of Egypt, which I loved. It was the history of the place that had made me want to go in the first place.

We booked some sightseeing trips. We went on an amazing safari in the desert and walked up big sand mountains and slid down, then we went on camels and saw how the poor people lived and how they cooked their food. Their bread was amazing.

* * *

Over the couple of weeks we were in Egypt, I met somebody who was very nice and wanted to stay in contact with me. When I got back home, I found out that he had not been completely honest with me about certain things.

When I went over and saw him again, I found out that he was Muslim. I was a Christian, so that wasn't going to work out, but I met a lot of good Christian men, including one who I actually stayed in touch with. I kept on going over to see him, and finally we got married in Egypt, Cairo.

It was hard because we wouldn't see each other for months at a time, and then eventually he came over. I was pregnant, and everything seemed against us. I found a lawyer here just in case things didn't work out, because there was a lot against us. I was working, but I didn't have any savings, and usually I would need to have money. The lucky thing was that he had money and savings.

When I saw the lawyer, it didn't look good. A lot of people were refused at the embassy. But when he had his interview, it was amazing. He believed that God intervened. The lady interviewing him said it didn't look good; he didn't even have the right paperwork with him. But she gave him a chance to go and get it. She laughed when she saw my bank account, but I believe she knew he was genuine.

She asked him a series of questions, like, "Why do you want to go?"

He asked her, "Why do you love your husband?" He also said he wanted to see his baby being born.

She granted him a visa. I believed that if it was from God, it was meant to be, and everything went easily. He seemed to be everything I wanted in a man. He was Christian like me, seemed to want the same things as me, and had a testimony of God.

I loved Egypt for how beautiful it was. We stayed in a nice hotel where we could see the pyramids from a distance. His family was amazing—the loveliest people you could meet. He was scared to bring me to them at first, because they didn't like the idea that I had been married before and had children, but they liked me a lot.

* * *

When he finally had his visa, I was so excited. My prayers had been answered, and he was coming home to me. He didn't like English weather much, but we were happy. I had our first son a couple of months after he came to England.

It was hard for him to get used to a different way of life and find a job. He was always comparing the money to Egyptian money, which was annoying at times. I had a new baby with not much sleep and was still working as a childminder. Fortunately, he eventually found a job.

I never got any sleep with my son, as he never slept. My husband would be out late working. I started to get depressed because I was so tired. He told me that he would find more work at two jobs so that I didn't have to work.

Things were good for a while, but then he started to become controlling and started being aggressive with our son. The baby was only a few months old, but my husband told me not to pick him up when he was crying and when he had finished his drink. When I went shopping, he would tell me not to and always compared the English money to Egyptian money. He started to argue, and we stopped getting on. When this happened, I would go shopping anyway. Then he would laugh, so everything would be all right.

Then his mum got sick. I had just come back from a holiday there but had to book a flight back for him to be with her. He was there for three months because his mum died. As one of the eldest, he had to sort everything out. I had to move to a new house on my own, doing everything myself as I had always done.

When he finally came back, things went okay between us, but he was depressed over his mother and was always in bed when he wasn't working, so I would be in a bad mood. Then he started staying up at night more and more on his laptop, saying that he had online work to do. One minute he was in a really good mood, funny and laughing, and the next minute he would be in a bad one. I felt disconnected from him at times.

I was pregnant with our second child, which he told me he didn't want. I distanced myself from him. He would always be out after work. He would talk for a bit and then be on his laptop all night, every night, until things got really bad. I realised that he was having an online affair. He actually told me she was his cousin in America, but I found out he had pictures of a girl who he had seen in America, not his cousin at all. He had slept with this woman he had met on the internet. It had been going on for quite some time.

I had actually found revealing images of them together in America. He told me he was visiting his cousin. I almost always knew there was something not right but didn't know what. He had locks on his laptop and phone but would try to assure me it was just so the kids didn't touch it and that he had important stuff on it.

He was hardly there for me and the boys. When my second son was born, I left him downstairs with his father because I was so tired from my first son, who was hyperactive. When I went to bed, he had to feed his son, so he actually formed a close bond with the boy. I was going through a lot at the time trying to get my oldest son diagnosed. He couldn't concentrate or sit still at school, and it took a long time.

Many nights, I felt alone and would cry. I'd never felt more alone being with somebody than not being with somebody. We would go on holiday together but end up arguing. We would just be nasty to each other, so I distanced myself so much that I didn't want anything to do with him. I always thought there was something going on, but I didn't have any proof. I prayed at night about it.

He kept encouraging me to go to Egypt and bring the kids, and then to live there. I just had bad feelings about that. I didn't want to go anywhere with him.

My husband didn't believe there was anything wrong with our eldest son. With my second son, he wasn't hyperactive, but I realised I never really saw him play with anything and he didn't respond when I was calling him. He was finally diagnosed with ASD (autism spectrum disorder), but still my husband wouldn't understand and was just so aggressive with him at times. Because he was so bright and clever, I think his father believed there was nothing wrong with him. I took courses to understand autism so that I could understand him more.

* * *

We had a lot of close-knit neighbours, which meant I didn't have much privacy. Our new home was nice, with four bedrooms, three stories, and three bathrooms, but no outside space for the children to play. I got on with most of my neighbours, but there were one or two noisy ones who would cause problems with other neighbours in the area.

One time, a new neighbour moved in next door to me. She seemed really nice and had lots of young children. Being a good neighbour, I asked her if she needed any help with moving in and cleaning. I did lots of things for her and looked after her baby and young ones. It was trying at times, and I started to see a change in her. One minute she would be really nice, the next really snappy. Then I found out she was a drug user.

I started to keep my distance from her, as she was becoming violent and aggressive. She would encourage her children to cause problems with my children. I saw this with my own eyes, and so did many of our neighbours. She was so childish, because she knew I was keeping my distance. There were so many arguments started with other neighbours. The police came out many times because she would get into violent arguments with many other neighbours.

I had my own problems to cope with. One time, it got so bad between me and my husband that I just wanted him to leave. He got violent with me and hit me. I was upset and on the phone to my sister, and she heard him being aggressive, so she phoned the police. He knew it was over. The police told him to leave and not come back to me.

We talked and decided that he would go to Egypt. I wanted to work things out, but I couldn't forgive him for what he did—cheating on me when he went to Egypt. I prayed and actually found a home exchange with somebody. I didn't need to look anywhere else; I just knew this was the house and everything would be fine. When I moved in, I felt peace there at last.

I started to decorate the house because it was such a mess. I finally got it how I wanted it to be, but it wasn't easy. I started to get help from my family. My daughter was recently married, and her husband helped a lot. My brothers lived nearby, which was great, as they helped me decorate the house.

My sister also lived nearby, which was nice at times. However, other times it would be a bit too much. I had a couple of brothers who were drug users because of the family situation when my mum died, and they looked to me for support. I felt like I was always held responsible for taking care of them. I felt sorry for them, especially as one of my brothers became homeless. I ended up taking him into my home, even though we only had a three-bedroom house.

I found him in my shed in the garden, and it was freezing cold outside, so I sorted out my utility room so he could stay in there. The utility room was small but enough for him, as there was a bed, a TV, and a cupboard for his clothes.

It was a challenge for me, as he didn't clean himself, and he smelt terrible. I had to run him a bath each day, but sometimes he would just make out he was having a bath. I bought him some clothes and made him food every night when he came home from work. Sometimes he would disappear for days. Other times he would do lots of jobs for me which I wasn't able to do myself. Still other times it would be extremely frustrating, as I didn't know how to help him. I would call a drug counsellor, but it didn't help at all.

Sometimes I would ask him when he was coming back. He would say he'd be back soon, but then he wouldn't come back for weeks. He found another place to live temporarily but would come back and stay for a little while and then take off again. I'd just had enough, as I had my own family to worry about, so I ended up packing his stuff and putting it in the shed for him to come and get it.

My eldest daughter had moved into her new house and had twin babies just before I moved. Once the twins were just under 1 year old, my daughter started going back to work. I was planning to look after them in a couple of months, from time to time.

I had to sort out my house again after my brother left. My other brother needed help. Soon after, one brother left another brother who had to leave his old place that he was renting with his girlfriend. His girlfriend moved back to Spain, so he had nowhere to live, as they shared the rent between them. He was also on drugs from time to time. But other times he would stop, so I thought he was clean at the time, so I took him in.

He was only meant to stay for a little while, around a week. It turned into weeks and then months. Instead of giving me money, he would do some jobs around the house. He was very clever at building and fixing things; however, he would take a lot of time to do the jobs for me. This was because he was working on the side at the same time.

One day, I found some needles in his belongings, so I told him I couldn't do this anymore, as I had children. I told him he had to leave, as it was dangerous. He then took some of his belongings and left. I was relieved. I just wanted my life back.

I finally stopped feeling responsible for my parents' mistakes with my brothers. What I wanted for myself and my family was to be at peace with no stress and no responsibility for others people's mistakes.

My ex-husband would come round from time to time. I

used to see him more than I did when we were together. He seemed to be doing more with the boys for a while, when the weather was nice. He would never take them anywhere; he would just come round and see them at my home. It was really awkward, so I ended up telling him that I'd just had enough. He needed to take the boys out and have them. He wouldn't listen; he would still just come around whenever he felt like it.

I felt like I couldn't get rid of him. It was like he was coming to see me, not just the boys, even though we were going through a divorce and had been separated for two years. He finally got the message and moved back to Egypt. He currently keeps in contact with his children and visits them and plans holidays with them. We get along well for the children's sake.

My oldest daughter would always help out. She was like a best friend and a partner to me. Work would take her away for a few days at a time, and her husband (who also worked) and I would sort out between our schedules to look after the twins. When I would look after the twins, we would have so much fun. I felt so much love for them, like my own children.

My oldest daughter is an air hostess for the Royal Air Force. My second oldest daughter is a chef and is very talented. My third daughter is currently doing travel and tourism. My eldest son has autism and is very good at memorizing numbers and breaking codes. My youngest son is very artistic, just like me. The challenges in my life have made my family stronger and closer.

I love all of my family so much, and I'm proud of all three of my daughters and my sons. We have wonderful holidays together, all of us. My family is my life and always will be. I feel I can say I've done something good. We all are very close; we all help each other and are very happy and supportive no matter what problems we have. So far, my faith and love of my family have been my life's purpose.

Mother and Father

This is me as a young child.

The newspaper article.

Printed in Great Britain
by Amazon